Illustrated Songbook

Music by Alan Menken • Lyrics by Stephen Schwartz

ISBN 0-7935-4655-9

WONDERLAND MUSIC COMPANY, INC. AND WALT DISNEY MUSIC COMPANY

DISTRIBUTED BY

7777 W. BLUEMOUND RD. P.O. BOX 13819 MILWAUKEE, WI 53213

CONTENTS

The Virginia Company

The Virginia Company

Music by **Alan Menken**
Lyrics by **Stephen Schwartz**

Like a sea shanty

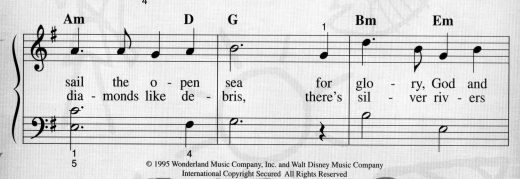

In six - teen hun - dred sev - en, we
beach - es of Vir - gin - ny, there's

sail the o - pen sea for glo - ry, God and
dia - monds like de - bris, there's sil - ver riv - ers

Bm   **Em**   **Am**   **G/B**

gold, and The Vir - gin - ia Com - pa -
flow and gold you pick right off a

C   **D7**   **G**

ny. For the New World is like
tree. With a nug - get for my

please turn the page…

The Virginia Company

Music by **Alan Menken**
Lyrics by **Stephen Schwartz**

In sixteen hundred seven
We sail the open sea
For glory, God and gold
And The Virginia Company
For the New World is like heaven
And we'll all be rich and free
Or so we have been told
By The Virginia Company
So we have been told
By The Virginia Company

For glory, God and gold
And The Virginia Company

On the beaches of Virginny
There's diamonds like debris
There's silver rivers flow
And gold you pick right off a tree
With a nugget for my Winnie
And another one for me
And all the rest will go
To The Virginia Company
It's glory, God and gold
And The Virginia Company

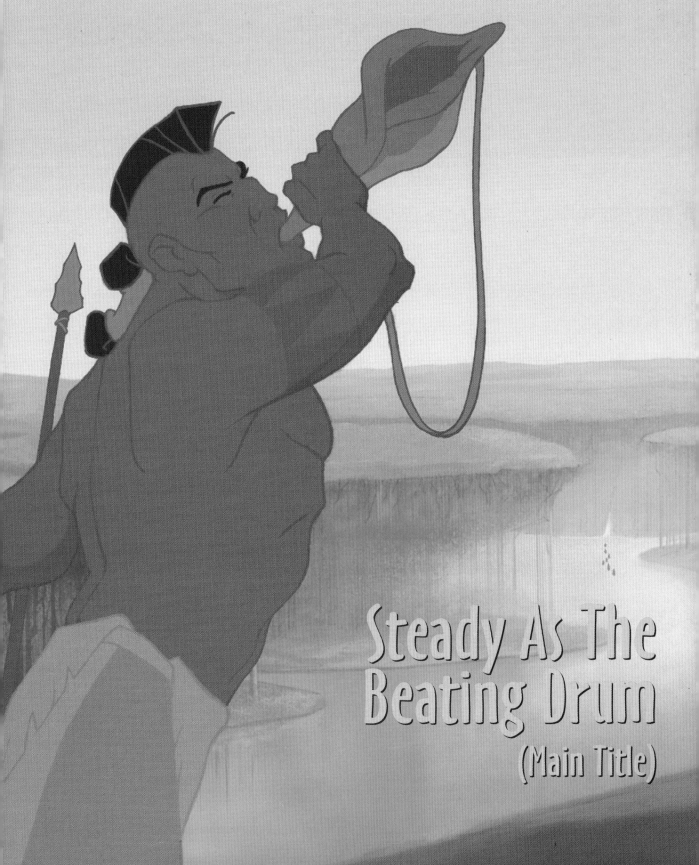

Steady As The Beating Drum
(Main Title)

Steady As The Beating Drum

(Main Title)

Music by **Alan Menken**
Lyrics by **Stephen Schwartz**

Moderately, steadily

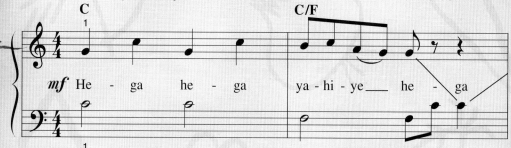

He - ga he - ga ya - hi - ye___ he - ga

ya - hi - ye___ ne - he he - ga.

Steady As The Beating Drum

Music by **Alan Menken**
Lyrics by **Stephen Schwartz**

WOMEN & MEN:
Hega hega ya-hi-ye hega
Ya-hi-ye ne-he hega
Hega hega ya-hi-ye hega
Ya-hi-ye ne-he hega

WOMEN:
Steady as the beating drum
Singing to the cedar flute
Seasons go and seasons come
Bring the corn and bear the fruit

WOMEN & MEN:
By the waters sweet and clean
Where the mighty sturgeon lives

Plant the squash and reap the bean
All the earth our mother gives

O Great Spirit, hear our song
Help us keep the ancient ways
Keep the sacred fire strong
Walk in balance all our days

Seasons go and seasons come
Steady as the beating drum
Plum to seed to bud to plum
(Hega ya-hi-ye hega)

Steady as the beating drum

Hega hega ya-hi-ye hega

Ya-hi-ye ne-he hega

Steady As The Beating Drum
(Reprise)

Music by **Alan Menken**
Lyrics by **Stephen Schwartz**

POWHATAN:

As the river cuts his path

Though the river's proud and strong

He will choose the smoothest course

That's why rivers live so long

They're steady...

As the steady beating drum

Just Around
The Riverbend

Just Around The Riverbend

With motion

Music by **Alan Menken**
Lyrics by **Stephen Schwartz**

Dm7/G **G** **Em**

know - ing what's a - round the riv - er - bend,

F **F/G** **Em/G**

wait-ing just a - round the riv - er - bend.

F/G **Em/G** **F/G** **G/F** **C/E** **F**

I look once more

please turn the page…

just a - round the riv - er - bend be - yond the shore,

where the gulls fly free. Don't know what for,

what I dream the day might send just a - round the riv - er - bend

for me.

Just Around The Riverbend

Music by **Alan Menken**
Lyrics by **Stephen Schwartz**

What I love most about rivers is:
You can't step in the same river twice
The water's always changing, always flowing
But people, I guess, can't live like that
We all must pay a price:
To be safe we lose our chance of ever knowing
What's around the riverbend
Waiting just around the riverbend

I look once more
Just around the riverbend
Beyond the shore
Where the gulls fly free
Don't know what for
What I dream the day might send
Just around the riverbend
For me...
Coming for me

I feel it there beyond those trees
Or right behind these waterfalls
Can I ignore that sound of distant drumming
For a handsome sturdy husband
Who builds handsome sturdy walls
And never dreams that something might be coming
Just around the riverbend?
Just around the riverbend

I look once more
Just around the riverbend
Beyond the shore
Somewhere past the sea
Don't know what for...
Why do all my dreams extend
Just around the riverbend?
Just around the riverbend...

Should I choose the smoothest course
Steady as the beating drum?
Should I marry Kocoum?
Is all my dreaming at an end?
Or do you still wait for me, Dream Giver
Just around the riverbend?

Listen With Your Heart

Listen With Your Heart

Mysteriously

Music by **Alan Menken**
Lyrics by **Stephen Schwartz**

© 1995 Wonderland Music Company, Inc. and Walt Disney Music Company
International Copyright Secured All Rights Reserved

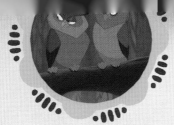

F   **Em**   **F**

stand.   Let it break up - on you   like a

Am   **F**   **G/F**   **F**   **G/F**

wave up - on the sand.
rall.

Am   **F**

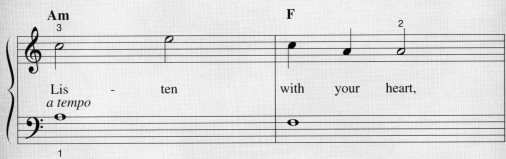

Lis - ten   with your heart,
a tempo

C   **D**   **Am**

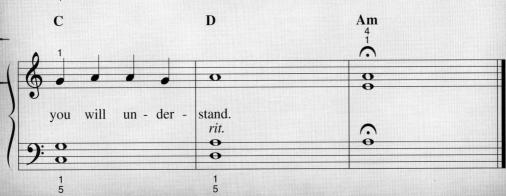

you will un - der - stand.
rit.

25

Listen With Your Heart

Music by **Alan Menken**
Lyrics by **Stephen Schwartz**

VOICE OF THE WIND:

Ay ay ay ya

Ay ay ya

GRANDMOTHER WILLOW:

Que que na-to-ra

You will understand

Listen with your heart

You will understand

Let it break upon you

Like a wave upon the sand

Listen with your heart

You will understand

VOICE OF THE WIND:

You will understand...

Mine, Mine, Mine

Mine, Mine, Mine

Music by **Alan Menken**
Lyrics by **Stephen Schwartz**

Madrigal style

all ya got in ya, boys, dig up Vir -

molto rit.

gin - ia, boys. Mine, boys, mine ev -'ry

a tempo

please turn the page…

C7   F   B♭   Gm7

moun - tain and dig,   boys, dig 'til ya

C7   A♭   D♭   Gm

drop. Grab a pick,   boys,   quick,

C   Dm   C/E

boys,   shove in a shov - el, un -

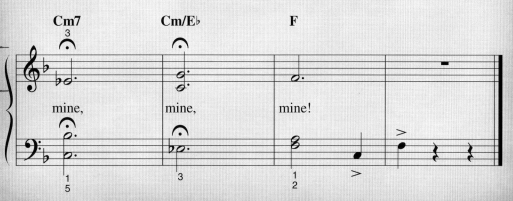

F   **B♭**   **F/C**

cov - er those lov - e - ly peb - bles that

C7   **Dm**   **G7**   **F/C**

spar - kle and shine. It's *rit.* gold and it's

Cm7   **Cm/E♭**   **F**

mine, mine, mine!

Mine, Mine, Mine

Music by **Alan Menken**
Lyrics by **Stephen Schwartz**

RATCLIFFE:
The Gold of Cortés
The jewels of Pizarro
Will seem like mere trinkets
By this time tomorrow
The gold we find here
Will dwarf them by far...
Oh, with all ya got in ya, boys
Dig up Virginia, boys

Mine, boys, mine ev'ry mountain
And dig, boys, dig 'til ya drop
Grab a pick, boys
Quick, boys
Shove in a shovel
Uncover those lovely
Pebbles that sparkle and shine
It's gold and it's mine, mine, mine!

ENGLISH SETTLERS:
Dig and dig and dig and diggety...
Dig and dig and dig and diggety...

WIGGINS:
Hey nonny nonny
Ho nonny nonny

RATCLIFFE:
Ooh, how I love it!
Riches for cheap!

WIGGINS:
There'll be heaps of it...

RATCLIFFE:
And I'll be on top of the heap!
My rivals back home...
It's not that I'm bitter
But think how they'll squirm
When they see how I glitter!
The ladies at court
Will be all a-twitter
The king will reward me
He'll knight me... no, *lord* me!

It's mine, mine, mine
For the taking
It's mine, boys
Mine me that gold!
With those nuggets dug...
It's glory they'll gimme
My dear friend King Jimmy
Will probably build me a shrine

RATCLIFFE & WIGGINS:
When all of the gold is mine!

ENGLISH SETTLERS:
Dig and dig and dig and diggety
Dig and dig and dig and diggety dig!

JOHN SMITH:
All of my life, I have searched for a land
Like this one...
A wilder, more challenging country
I couldn't design
Hundreds of dangers await
And I don't plan to miss one
In a land I can claim
A land I can tame
The greatest adventure is mine

RATCLIFFE & ENGLISH SETTLERS:
Keep on working, lads...   Mine
Don't be shirking, lads... Find a mother lode
Mine, boys, mine   Then find another load!
Mine me that gold!   Dig! Dig! and diggety
Gold!   Dig! Dig! and diggety
Beautiful gold   Dig! Dig! for that gold

ALL:
Make this island
My land!

RATCLIFFE:
Make the mounds big, boys
I'd help ya to dig, boys
But I've got this crick in my spine

SMITH:
This land we behold...

RATCLIFFE:
This beauty untold...

SMITH:
A man can be bold!

RATCLIFFE:
It *all* can be sold!

RATCLIFFE & ENGLISH SETTLERS:
And the gold   So go for the gold
Is...   We know which is here
                  All the riches here
Mine!   From this minute
Mine!   This land and what's in it is
Mine!   Mine!

Dig and dig and diggety dig!
Hey nonny nonny nonny it's mine!

Colors Of The Wind

Colors Of The Wind

Music by **Alan Menken**
Lyrics by **Stephen Schwartz**

Moderately

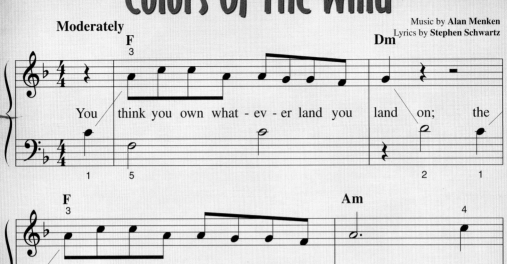

You think you own what-ev-er land you land on; the

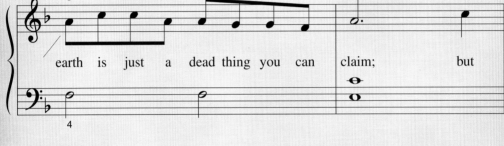

earth is just a dead thing you can claim; but

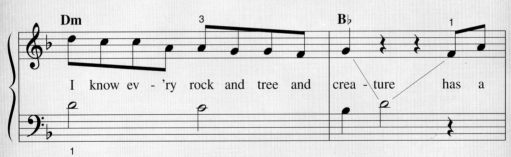

I know ev-'ry rock and tree and crea-ture has a

life, has a spir-it, has a name. You

F   **Dm**

think the on - ly peo - ple who are   peo - ple   are the

F   **Am**

peo - ple who look and think like   you,   but

Dm   **B**♭

if you walk the foot-steps of a   strang - er   you'll learn

please turn the page…

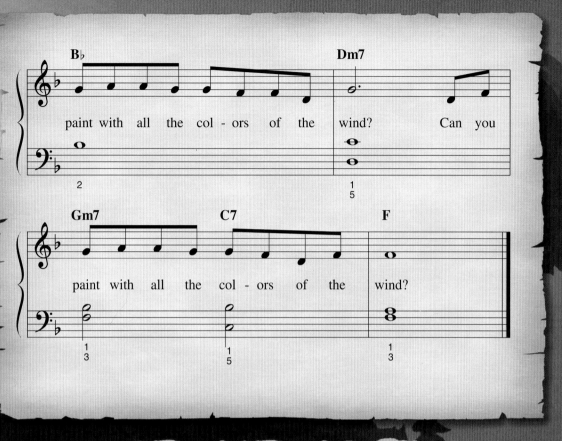

paint with all the col - ors of the wind? Can you

paint with all the col - ors of the wind?

Colors Of The Wind

Music by **Alan Menken**
Lyrics by **Stephen Schwartz**

POCAHONTAS:
You think I'm an ignorant savage
And you've been so many places
I guess it must be so
But still I cannot see
If the savage one is me
How can there be so much that
you don't know?
You don't know...

You think you own whatever
land you land on
The earth is just a dead thing
you can claim
But I know ev'ry rock and
tree and creature
Has a life, has a spirit,
has a name

You think the only people
who are people
Are the people who look and
think like you
But if you walk the footsteps
of a stranger
You'll learn things you never
knew you never knew

Have you ever heard the wolf cry
to the blue corn moon
Or asked the grinning bobcat
why he grinned?
Can you sing with all the
voices of the mountain?
Can you paint with all the
colors of the wind?
Can you paint with all the
colors of the wind?

Come run the hidden pine trails
of the forest
Come taste the sun-sweet
berries of the earth
Come roll in all the riches
all around you
And for once, never wonder what
they're worth

The rainstorm and the river
are my brothers
The heron and the otter are
my friends
And we are all connected
to each other
In a circle, in a hoop that
never ends

How high does the
sycamore grow?
If you cut it down, then
you'll never know

And you'll never hear the wolf cry
to the blue corn moon
For whether we are white or
copper-skinned
We need to sing with all the
voices of the mountain
Need to paint with all the
colors of the wind
You can own the earth and still
All you'll own is earth until
You can paint with all the
colors of the wind

Savages
(Part 1)

Savages
(Part 1)

Music by **Alan Menken**
Lyrics by **Stephen Schwartz**

English Settlers:
They're sav-ag-es! Sav-ag-es! *Ratcliffe:* Bare-ly e-ven hu-man!
sav-ag-es! Sav-ag-es! Bare-ly e-ven hu-man!

English Settlers:
Sav-ag-es! Sav-ag-es! *Ratcliffe:* Drive them from our shore! They're
Sav-ag-es! Sav-ag-es! *Powhatan:* Kill-ers at the core. They're
Kekata:

not like you and me which means they must be e - vil.
dif-fer-ent from us which means they can't be trust - ed.

We must sound the drums of war. *English Settlers:* They're
Powhatan: We must sound the drums of war. *Native Americans:* They're

Savages
(Part 1)

Music by **Alan Menken**
Lyrics by **Stephen Schwartz**

RATCLIFFE:
What can you expect
From filthy little heathens?
Here's what you get when races
are diverse
Their skin's a hellish red
They're only good when dead
They're vermin, as I said
And worse —

ENGLISH SETTLERS:
They're savages! Savages!

RATCLIFFE:
Barely even human

ENGLISH SETTLERS:
Savages! Savages!

RATCLIFFE:
Drive them from our shore!
They're not like you and me
Which means they must be evil
We must sound the drums of war!

ENGLISH SETTLERS:
They're savages! Savages!
Dirty shrieking devils!
Now we sound the drums of war!

POWHATAN:
This is what we feared
The paleface is a demon
The only thing they feel at
all is greed

KEKATA:
Beneath that milky hide
There's emptiness inside

NATIVE AMERICANS:
I wonder if they even bleed
They're savages! Savages!
Barely even human
Savages! Savages!

POWHATAN:
Killers at the core

KEKATA:
They're different from us
Which means they can't
be trusted

POWHATAN:
We must sound the drums of war

NATIVE AMERICANS:
They're savages! Savages!
First we deal with this one
Then we sound the drums of war!

ENGLISH SETTLERS:
Savages! Savages!

BEN:
Let's go kill a few, men!

NATIVE AMERICANS:
Savages! Savages!

RATCLIFFE:
Now it's up to you, men!

ALL:
Savages! Savages!
Barely even human!
Now we sound the drums of war!

Savages
(Part 2)

Savages
(Part 2)

Music by **Alan Menken**
Lyrics by **Stephen Schwartz**

In strict tempo

Ratcliffe: This will be the day... (*Let's go men!*)

Powhatan: This will be the morn-ing. (*Bring out the prisoner.*)

English Settlers and Native Americans: We will see them dy - ing in the dust. **Pocahontas:** I don't know what I can do,

still I know I've got to try. **English Settlers:** Now we make 'em pay.

Savages
(Part 2)

Music by **Alan Menken**
Lyrics by **Stephen Schwartz**

RATCLIFFE:
This will be the day...
(Let's go men!)

POWHATAN:
This will be the morning...
(Bring out the prisoner)

ENGLISH SETTLERS &
NATIVE AMERICANS:
We will see them dying in
the dust

POCAHONTAS:
I don't know what I can do
Still I know I've got to try

ENGLISH SETTLERS:
Now we make 'em pay

POCAHONTAS:
Eagle, help my feet to fly

NATIVE AMERICANS:
Now without a warning

POCAHONTAS:
Mountain, help my heart be great

ENGLISH SETTLERS &
NATIVE AMERICANS:
Now we leave 'em blood and
bone and rust

POCAHONTAS:
Spirits of the earth and sky...

ENGLISH SETTLERS &
NATIVE AMERICANS:
It's them or us

POCAHONTAS:
Please don't let it be too late...

ENGLISH SETTLERS &
NATIVE AMERICANS:
They're just a bunch of
filthy, stinking
Savages! Savages!
Demons! Devils!

RATCLIFFE:
Kill them!

ENGLISH SETTLERS &
NATIVE AMERICANS:
Savages! Savages!

RATCLIFFE:
What are we waiting for?

ALL:
Destroy their evil race
Until there's not a trace left

POCAHONTAS:
How loud are the drums of war?

ALL:
We will sound the drums of war
(Savages! Savages!)
Now we sound the drums of war
(Savages! Savages!)

RATCLIFFE:
Now we see what comes
Of trying to be chums

NATIVE AMERICANS:
Now we sound the
drums...of...war!

ENGLISH SETTLERS:
Of course it means the
drums...of...war!

POCAHONTAS:
Is the death of all I love
Carried in the drumming of war?